AF394554

Platform

Simone Brewster

Platform

Simone Brewster

the DESIGN MUSEUM

Introduction

Danielle Thom

Mammy side-table, 2010

Designer. Artist. Polymath. Educator. Mother. Woman. Simone Brewster is all of these, and more. Born and raised in London of Jamaican and Trinidadian parents, she originally trained in architecture, studying at The Bartlett School of Architecture. I first encountered her creative practice in 2018, as a curator tasked with assembling a collection of contemporary craft for the Museum of London (re-launched as the London Museum in 2026).

The London Museum is now the home of Brewster's *The Mammy* (2010) – a powerful indictment of misogynoir in the guise of a side-table, the top of which rests upon a disembodied breast and thighs in ebonised tulipwood. The entire piece functions as a metaphor for Black female labour, the eponymous 'Mammy' stereotype on which so much white exploitation has rested. Since then, Brewster's practice has evolved across different media, and explored new avenues of identity and culture. It starts, though, with architecture and with London.

Brewster's architectural training is most apparent in her earliest works – primarily jewellery, vessels and furniture – which obey a harmonious and balanced geometry. They can be seen as little structures for urbanising the body and the domestic interior. Her jewellery, especially, hovers somewhere between Brutalism and Streamline Moderne in its simplicity. The aptly named 'Metropolis' range (2015) mimics the towering symmetrical forms of Fritz Lang's 1927 film of the same name, while the Major Architects ring wittily mimics the chaise longue designs of Le Corbusier and Mies van der Rohe. In a medium coded as feminine and decorative, she turns canonical designs by white men into miniature objects.

Stepping away from the modernist canon, Brewster's 'Africa Utopia' series (2016) uses elegant, minimal fan-like shapes in a way that recalls pre-colonial Yoruba and Igbo architecture. These jewellery pieces are imposing in their aspect despite the size of the medium. This dichotomy is characteristic of Brewster's work, which is at once intimate and monumental. It has the specificity

Major Architects ring, 2009

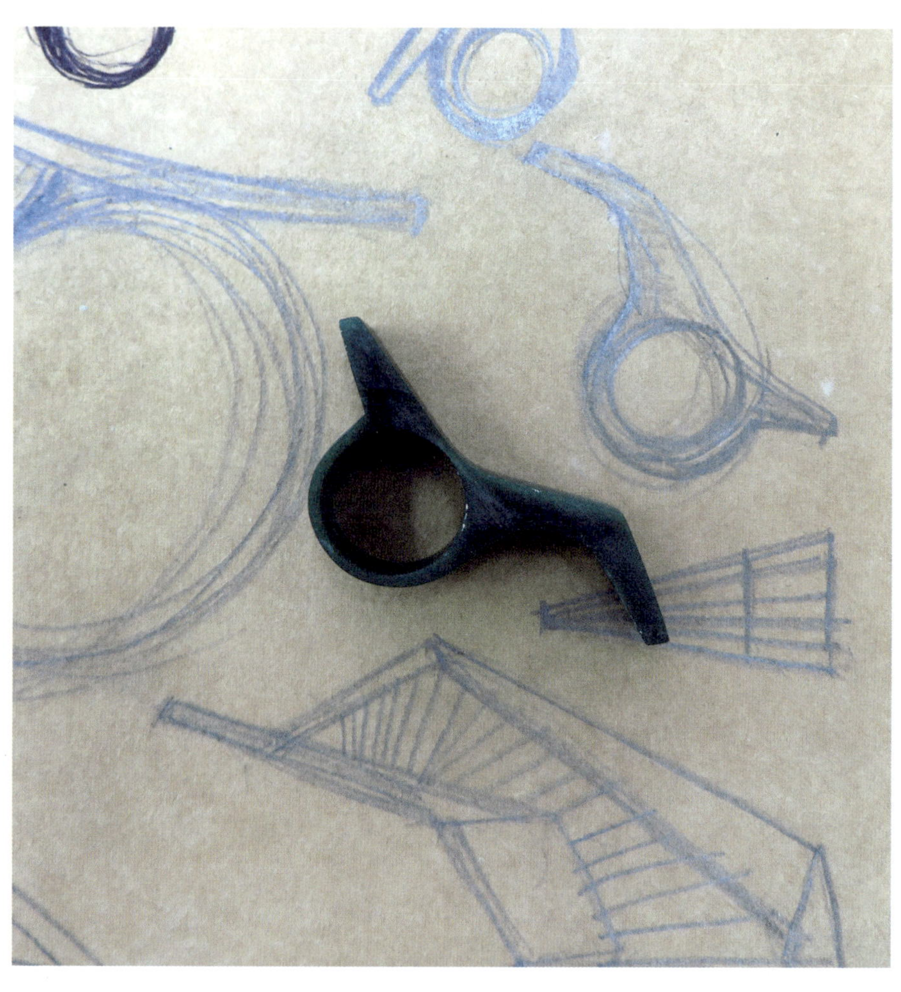

Above: Major Architects ring prototype, 2009

  Overleaf: Negress chaise longue, 2010

of autobiography, while at the same time drawing confidently on global histories of race, colonialism, gender and sexuality. Works such as *The Mammy* – and its companion *The Negress* (2010), now in the collection of the Smithsonian's National Museum of African American History and Culture in Washington, D.C. – embody this dichotomy, quite literally. Their composition and materiality speak both to Brewster's own lived experience as a Black woman, a person of Afro-Caribbean heritage whose ancestors would have been enslaved, and to the institutionalised and systematised physical and economic exploitation of Black women's bodies. More pointedly, they reference Brewster's experience and identity as a Black woman in London, a city whose economic and political might is historically founded on the profits of colonialism and the subsequent reception of diasporic cultural influences. Put simply, the history of Black Londoners is inextricably entwined with that of the British empire, of slavery, and of trade. Brewster's works have engaged with this painful past in both their form and materiality.

Both *Mammy* and *Negress* are ebonised – that is to say, the underlying pale wood has been treated with a darkening agent to mimic the hue and sheen of ebony. The ebony tree itself, *Diospyros crassiflora*, is endemic to West Africa. Today it is an endangered species thanks to centuries of logging for the European luxury furniture trade; a form of plunder which existed alongside the human plunder of the slave trade. The wood of the tree, therefore, is no longer a viable option for a designer such as Brewster, herself a descendent of the African diaspora via the Caribbean. She uses the ebonisation technique to mimic Black skin, giving further resonance to the breast- and limb-like forms, but this ebonisation remains a surface layer on top of the tulipwood.

Whiteness overlaid with blackness, these material strata create a palimpsest which echoes the cultural diversity of Brewster's London, drawing in layers upon layers of material, economic and personal histories. Brewster used wood elsewhere in her practice, juxtaposing its physical and semiotic qualities to

similarly profound effect. The Afro combs which constitute *Crown* (2023) are made from black palm and sapele wood. As the form of each comb celebrates a specific African hairstyle, its material calls back to the biodiversity of West and Central Africa – natural hair embraced by natural landscape. In the 'Tropical Noire' series of vessels (2015), the architectural forms which characterise Brewster's jewellery are continued, but here are realised in a combination of maple and, again, ebonised tulipwood. The vessels themselves are conscious recollections of West African sculpture, with stepped decorative rings akin to the ring collars on certain Benin bronze heads, and elongated necks atop broad bases like a traditional water gourd. Yet they also echo the symmetrical, industrialised motifs of Art Deco architecture. The wood is what roots these vessels in an African context, and the effect of the whole is one of Afrofuturist opulence: powerful, authentic, modern.

The medium of the vessel is significant in other ways, for it is inherently a carrier, a void waiting to be filled; in the case of a water gourd, it sustains life and nourishment. In this respect it can be tied to another important theme in Brewster's work – that of femininity and motherhood. While the two are by no means synonymous, in her own lived experience they are connected. Revisiting the ideas first broached in *Mammy* and *Negress*, the *Maid* table (2011) again uses the motif of abstracted female parts as a mode of support.

This time, however, the tabletop is made of glass, connoting vulnerability and transparency. Is it the vulnerability of the hypothetical woman whose body supports the table? Or the vulnerability of systemic racism and sexism, which can be combatted more effectively when properly exposed? In this sense, the piece marks an evolution in the narrative function of Brewster's work, shifting from a critique of what has been, to an analysis of what could be. Those explorations of the female form which characterised her earlier work are also continued in Brewster's practice as a painter; a practice which grew in relative solitude during the COVID-19 lockdowns of 2020. Not so much bodies but disembodied fragments are now rendered in ever more abstract forms – a curved line suggesting a breast or a buttock, at once vulnerable and assertive. In their scale and their subject matter, the paintings serve as an essential counterbalance to Brewster's recent step into architectural commissions for the public realm, such as *Spirit of Place* (2023) and *Temple of Relics* (2025). These latter interventions scale up the vessel into a series of monumental obelisks, drawing upon classical architectural principles to create spaces which feel comfortingly ancient, calling back across time to a distant past of ancestors and lost ritual.

In the universality of her practice, Brewster defies simple categorisation when exploring the timeless ideas of heritage, identity and womanhood. Though her works approach a kind of mythical 'everywoman', Brewster can only ever be herself: unique. In the following pages her complex interplay of materiality, craft and identity are explored in full. ■

Another Point of
Return

Simone Brewster in conversation
with Thomas Aquilina

Still from the film *Passages*, commissioned for the 2026 PLATFORM
exhibition at the Design Museum

Thomas Aquilina

In this conversation I'd like us to think about lines of enquiry in your work through three possible points of return. First, around institutional return (partly by us having this conversation in this building at The Bartlett), second, a return to heritage and, third, a return to the discipline of architecture. This cyclical idea of 'return' draws on a small text I wrote in *Sound Advice* (2021), about how to occupy multiple places simultaneously. I think your work inherently does this. To begin, can you take me back to being an architecture student at The Bartlett and how you navigated that formative experience?

Simone Brewster

I didn't really fit in when I was here. For various reasons. I may have even been too young. I didn't do a foundation course, I came straight here. Very Caribbean. 'You got the grades, they let you in. Why do you want to do a foundation course?' 'Ok mum and dad!' When I left, getting through the other side was a huge learning practice. I survived. I was in Unit 2, the making unit, and I'd just go in the workshop to make and play with materials, do plaster casting and welding. But it was also really the first time I was aware I was Black. That sounds dumb, because I've been Black my whole life. But it was the first time I'd been in an institution and place that made me aware of it. It really made me understand if I put my mind to something, I can do it: 'I know how you see me. Let me show you who I really am'. It's like taking control of your own narrative and using the work to do that.

TA

I had a similar experience, in Edinburgh, when I properly realised my difference – my Blackness. But in realising that, it allowed me to see more clearly. With this in mind, in what ways did your practice evolve from this architecture beginning?

SB

I think I have developed a question-led practice where I am led
through the questions that get me to create, as opposed to already
predicting what the answer is, if that makes sense. A turning point
came for me when I was a student at the Royal College of Art, on
a trip with my tutors Tom Dixon and Martino Gamper to Nigeria.
We were led, in Nigeria, by a sculptor, Olu Omoda. He invited us
to his workshop, took us to Yaba Technology (YABATECH), and he
partnered us with entities to put on a show at the British Council
in Lagos. I was totally energised. I made two seats, one in the
outfit of a man and one in the outfit of a woman. I made the metal
frames, welded it, and took it to local craftsmen and local weavers.
That was the first point of my real practice.

TA

So, your practice on display at the Design Museum is through this
framework of 'platforms'. I suppose there are many ways to see
what constitutes a platform, but my way of understanding your
approach is through a cultivation of new forms and these forms
generate new meanings. I wonder what that means to you?

SB

I saw the Chris Ofili show in 2010 where he said, 'I make the work
that doesn't exist in the world'. And I thought, 'That's it!' After
the exhibition I had this energy, this crystallisation that Gabriel
Klasmer was saying to me at the RCA. He said, 'You want to say
something, but you just don't know what you want to say!' I think
he could see my frustration, and he could see my skills. Even
though my products were good, it wasn't the real work. He said to
me, 'I don't know what you want to say or why you're not saying
it. Maybe you're not ready to say it yet and this isn't the space'.
I didn't know what to do with it at the time. After the Chris Ofili
show, I knew: 'It's time to say it'. That's what a platform is. This is
how I can talk about what I want to talk about.

Above: Chris Ofili, *Triple Beam Dreamer*, 2001-2. Acrylic, oil, leaves, glitter, polyester resin, map pins and elephant dung on canvas. Discussing his 2010 show at Tate Britain, Chris Ofili said 'I make the work that doesn't exist in the world'. These words and this artwork inspired Brewster to make her more conceptual works, *Negress* and *Mammy*.

TA

I also wonder if platform is another, perhaps more appropriate, way to think about a manifesto. It was Lebbeus Woods' manifesto, *War and Architecture*, that really influenced you, is that right?

SB

Yes. I love Lebbeus Woods. He caught this feeling of wanting to change the world through design, through architecture, but also not fitting in or not wanting to be held into one way of doing, and he seemed a bit angry. I could relate to that energy he had.

TA

Of all the different scales of work that you explored, which piece provided the largest platform and why? And to who?

SB

The pivotal works are *Negress* and *Mammy*, which are the foundational stones of my whole practice. It was important to me to make *Negrita*, so this had presence in the Design Museum show. It does many things – it is a craft object, it can be appreciated in design elements, but it speaks about society, things we don't speak about in design objects. But then there are projects like *Spirit of Place*, which is important. This is the danger of labels, in making work you do box yourself in. People thought of me a certain way. What London Design Festival and Amorim [cork processing group, partner at the Festival] gave me was an opportunity to say 'but remember, this is what I can actually do if you give me the opportunity, the platform'.

TA

You describe these two projects in different scales. One is more about the object and one is architectural. I would like to speak to you more about this. I genuinely believe that architecture is always contextual. And I wonder if you think about the object in

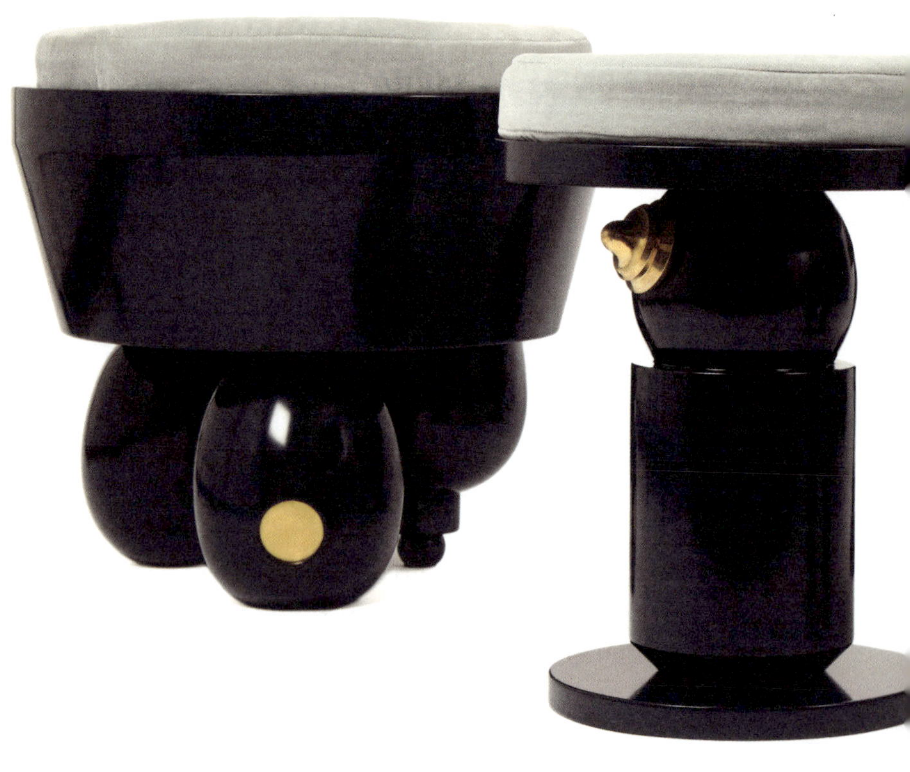

 Large 3-breasted stool, Single breast stool, Head stool, and 3-Limb stool, Servant Collection, 2018

opposition, and if the object can be contextless. How do you think through context at different scales?

SB
I learnt more about context through making. When I first made *Negress* and *Mammy*, the context was to make a furniture piece. For me, that was still a piece of furniture, but I learned that through tackling those issues the context diverts to art. It becomes an art piece when you have the tension of sitting on that seat. 'Sit on it, then.' When you understand what's going on, the tension builds up and you don't want to sit on it. That's a performance, that's an art piece. I learnt about contextualisation in my work, and I learned a lot from making that piece. I understood that this is when this 'intimate architecture' really started to make sense for me. Every object has a narrative. How we combine objects builds a narrative. We can build a space of just objects; we don't need four walls and a roof. Therefore architecture can be created through an assemblage of objects. That's my learning.

TA
If my provocation was to say an object itself is contextless, in a sense *Spirit of Place* had no home – but the context you're evoking is deeper, richer. It's connected to the forest and the materiality. So actually your argument back to me is something about the lens of context you're speaking through. Which is a very architectural way to think, but you're offering up a kind of a broadened inquiry.

SB
But this is even in the name, *genius loci* – spirit of place. It's about the historic meaning of that term, which is a spirit of a location that gave it its presence and feeling.

TA
Then if we think about this naming of things... Thinking about

language and how language plays a role in the projects, how do you allow yourself to employ at times racist language in naming some of the works?

SB
Sometimes when I name a thing, it's very clear what I have to do to achieve what I want. I'm trying to talk about these very difficult things. We call it by its name. And then we can't hide from it and pretend it's something else, even if I want to, because sometimes it's easier to just not talk about it. It's not always comfortable to talk about, even for me. But if it's called a thing, you're not going be able to put that away in a box. You're just gonna have to confront it.

TA
I've been feeling very nervous and in suspense about the impending catastrophe of Hurricane Melissa as we sit here today. Given that we share a Jamaican heritage, I wonder, what does it mean to make work at this time of turbulence? Not just this real feeling of disaster that is crashing towards Jamaica, but in this current era of omnicrisis.

SB
Part of me making my real work, *Negress* and *Mammy* and all these pieces, was the realisation that the world was full of work that was beautiful but also pointless. Going to Milan, do we need another rotational chair? Probably not. We need work that is going to say more and to do more. And now I'm at the point where I don't feel like my work is pointless, but the problems are bigger.

TA
What makes you keep making?

SB
I make my work because I think it deserves to be made. They were

inviting other people to do shows but they weren't inviting me.
So I started FLOCK with other female creatives because I'm like,
'You're just waiting for someone to pick you, let's pick ourselves,
okay?' And then I did a show for the Royal College of Art called
RCA Black. A letter was written to the Dean of the School and the
Guardian newspaper saying, 'How dare you talk about the Royal
College of Art in this way'. And so people don't know what to
do with me. Right now, I feel like I am growing. I am being giving
opportunities and platforms I didn't have before, which means the
impact being made is just greater. I care about the fact that the
work is made. I think people see me as a rebel and they don't really
know what to do with me. There are things in my sketchbooks from
2008 that I am only realising now, because I couldn't make it on
my livelihood at that moment in time. I care about the fact that the
work is made.

TA
There's another point of return…

SB
100%. If you go through my sketchbooks, it's going in circles.
One sketch became a hieroglyphic in *Temple of Relics*, that idea
was planted then. Ideas planted in 2010 that I am making now.
Previously I didn't have the opportunity to realise a fifth of my
ideas in the world. I'd like to continue realising and evidencing
what I imagine. There are others who have the freedom and the
opportunity to realise them, so why shouldn't I?

Opposite: Temple of Relics, 2025
Following pages: Concept sketches for Temple of Relics, 2024,
and general view of Temple of Relics, Summer Pavillion, 2025

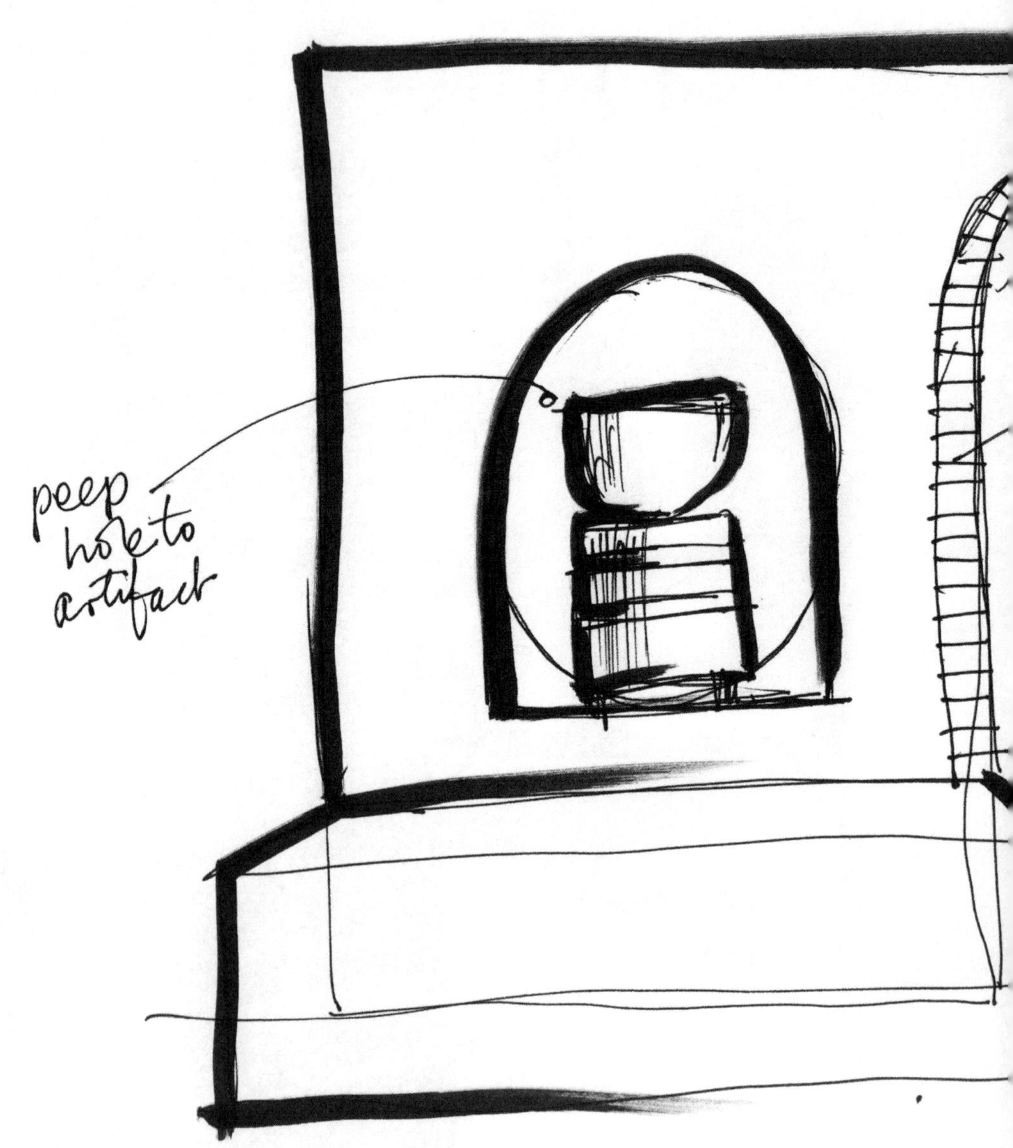
peep
hole to
artifact

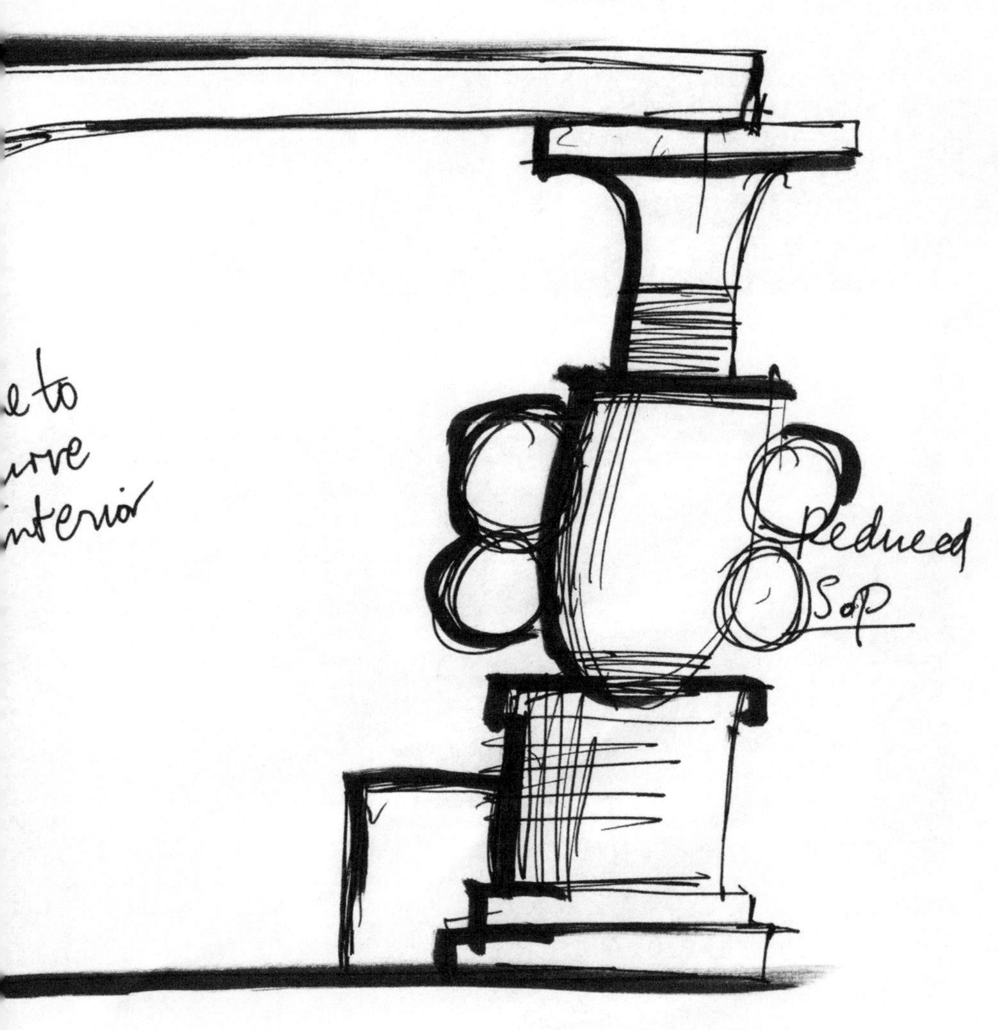
e to
rve
interior
Reduced
Sop

Passages

Hadeel Eltayeb

Concept sketches for Maid screen, 2009

*As I re-entered education, I surrounded myself with
neoclassical architecture – grand facades, big steps – the
environment that, in this country, is curiously mandatory for
those entering academia. I became a caryatid, Greek column,
passive stone woman, outside the Crypt gallery, supporting
the heavy stone Portico. (Rosa-Johan Uddoh)*

Telling someone about a dream often begins with recreating
a surreal image: 'I saw myself…' While dreaming has no borders,
Simone Brewster's architectural ambitions exposed her to working
within structural constraints. As a young designer, she re-imagined
her role in institutions with rigid categories to accommodate the
making she was interested in, visualising it before it became real.
Visionary designer Virgil Abloh spoke compellingly about making
design exciting for both 'the purist and the tourist' – embracing
the design aficionado who holds Dieter Ram's *Ten Principles For
Good Design* sacred, but also the tourist, as either the deliberate
or unwitting rule-breaker. Being a tourist, and thereby taking a
more ambulatory and less direct route, can be a richer education in
design. Brewster was always a rule-breaker. Rather than following
one design tradition, she created a perspective born of many.

Brewster borrows from design codes of modernism she
learned studying architecture, but invites in plural influences,
shared histories and cultural identities reflective of her story,
from Trinidad to Tottenham. She celebrates vernacular objects
and symbols associated with the Black diaspora. Her flair in
re-appropriation and agency makes delicately crafted, functional
objects out of her rich assemblage of cultural references.
Her design thinking translates elements across disciplines to
create functional designs, her sketches calibrating scale and
perspective. As a young RCA graduate of product design, in 2007
she drew on architect Lebbeus Woods' 1993 manifesto, *War and
Architecture*, for her graduate statement. Two lines are prescient
of her long return to architecture after a career that pivoted to

sculpture, product design and painting: 'I declare war on all icons and finalities, on all histories that would chain me with my own falseness./I am a constructor of worlds, a sensualist who worships the flesh.' As a young designer, Brewster held a self-awareness of social codes – how she was expected to speak, think and dress to conform to the expectations of professional design. But rather than conforming, her journey changed when, instead of following the status quo, she chose to follow her curiosities, creating a path that is liberatory and imaginative.

A quest to rediscover where she finds value drives Brewster's story. She sees beauty and luxury in materials that are often dismissed as common and less valuable. Studying at the RCA under contemporary designers such as Tom Dixon, Hannes Koch and Martino Gamper, she analysed what qualities made objects desirable. The attention-seeking appeal of iridescent objects suited materials like diamonds or gold. But in her design practice, the common timber is worthy of serious (re)consideration. She appreciates its variety, from the dark wood hand-carved African sculptures collected by her parents to her grandfather's hand-built kitchen in Jamaica, constructed from rippled monochrome mahoe wood in his garden. Brewster's first jewellery collection was named 'Ebony Revolution' (2009), implying the perspective shift required to make wood high-end. She assessed wood like a diamond, cutting along the surface to expose the grain, embracing its texture. Sustainably sourcing woods such as ebony, mango wood, limewood and sapele, she recycled materials, memories, emotions. Over time, she discovered that beautiful design suggests we think about how objects make us feel as much as how well they work.

Brewster's unique fusion of architecture and sculptural forms allows for multiple readings. Her subject matter is as fluid as her practice. She moves between polarities and leans into their slippage. She blurs the boundaries between structural and objective violence, layers historical time with memory and

38　　Wilfredo Lam, *The Murmur (Le Bruit)*, 1943

unfolds the realm of dreams and emotions, all at once. Brewster's designs are sites of exploration that give durational forms of time a spatial dimension. Cultural theorist Justin Smith coined the term 'Afrovisualism', defined as the theorisation and critical engagement of Black aesthetics, placing artists and theorists in conversation across time and space. After spending several months with Brewster's work, I could see how her designs animate time, remixing and reappropriating Black aesthetics from historical and contemporary sources. Artworks such as Tarsila do Amaral's *La Negra* (1923), Wilfredo Lam's *The Murmur* (1943) and, most notably, Chris Ofili's *Triple Beam Dreamer* (2001–2) can be read in Brewster's visual language. Her *Crown* combs, for example, are tributes to the diversity of hair customs in Africa, from Northeastern Congo to Nigeria. Hairstyles carried nuanced meaning, offering protection by identifying a tribe or a member of royalty, or marking a woman in mourning.

Vernacular architecture is also referenced in objects such as Brewster's 'Tropical Noire' series of vessels (2015). The intentional misspelling of the French word *noir* to feminise the singular form, the vessels carrying life-giving water, and the sculpted curvature of the forms all symbolise the integral force of women in their communities. The colours are inspired by West African patterns, from black-and-white textiles to the painted houses of Kassena people in Ghana and Burkina Faso.

They evoke bodies of water used by tribes, connecting people to a rhythm of seasons, a way of life. Brewster designed the vessels as tower-like monuments, a pointed nod to the enduring colonial legacies in Africa carried through language. Kenyan philosopher John Mbiti wrote that African religions see time as a never-ending cycle, distant from Western ideas of linear time indicating development and progress. Brewster's vessels transcend contemporary design and become mythic storytelling, timeless objects symbolic of pre-western African spirituality, where time is measured by seasons and ceremonies. As well

40   Tropical Noire vessel, 2014

as experimenting with time references, Brewster is fascinated
by bodily forms and how they are fragmented or fetishised by
society's gaze. By embracing and confronting womanhood
and Blackness in her designs, from painting to furniture, she
interrogates their societal erasure. Displaying these works has
raised interesting discussions within the museum, such as *Are
we looking at a nude if there is no body?* Brewster's works spark a
dialogue about presence and erasure, desire and intimacy. In her
painting series 'Woman in Parts', she critiques societal depictions
of women, in hopes of liberation. Her works refiguring how Black
women are represented – *The Negress*, *Negrita* and *The Mammy*
– place them in the loci of Afrofuturism, a cultural aesthetic which
animates time and expresses agency, identity and freedom for
Black people through works visualising liberation.

In 2010 Brewster was struck by eighteenth-century figurines in
a museum's collection, made by plantation owners to flaunt sugar,
banana and coffee fortunes. These objects turned Black women's
bodies into exoticised comical props, trapped in colonial fantasies.
Brewster designed the *Mammy* side-table and the *Negress* chaise
longue to draw attention to the irony of those museum 'treasures'.
The names are provocative, conjuring stereotypes reducing
women to symbolic fragments. The most fetishised body parts
– breasts, thighs – bear the weight of the structures. This series
emphasises the nipple as a symbol of eroticism but also of a
twisted motherhood forced on enslaved Black women.

An Afrofuturist reading could perhaps be a crucible for the
complex subjectivity in Brewster's work, when, not seeing herself
reflected in the design world around her, she constructed new
realities – past, present and future. She held an awareness of the
designer's role in constructing the future. In employing racially
charged imagery, Brewster's symbolism recalls artist Betye Saar's
Black Crows In Whites Section Only (1972), a work which contains
a Black child next to a Ku Klax Klan effigy. Like Saar, Brewster
invokes stereotypical images of Black bodies to liberate them from

passivity. She reappropriates historicised forms using influences such as surrealism and cubism, contributing new Black identities in the process. Her exploration of the body invites a cubist perspective (another deconstructionist approach), separating and analysing an object from multiple views, reassembling a personhood that has been maligned. She provokes the passive onlooker by making us part of an encounter with these objects; furniture made for our service. Facing towards the viewer at different angles, the eye of the nipple arrests us with its gaze. Unfulfilled desire sharpens into something darker that touch can no longer replicate – it becomes obsession.

Simone's surreal contortions of the Black body give obsession a form, crystallising supressed fear and desire, the tension between desire and violence. Brewster is empowered as both designer and subject to confront representations of maligned Blackness and to provoke discussion, forcing us to confront why institutions still collect and display racist imagery at all. Brewster's surrealist constructions go beyond showcasing societal fragilities in her designs. They also appeal to dreams as domains of agency, a joyful freedom where our emotions dictate our surroundings. She imbues emotions and heightened sensuality to objects in dream-like scales: rugs that look like they are dripping paint, urban spaces transformed into spiritual sanctuaries.

Temple of Relics (2025), designed as a summer pavilion in London's Shoreditch, presented a bright, generous infrastructure for people to dwell within the fast-paced city swarming with corporate banks and grey suits. The antithesis of neo-classical architecture, it celebrated Brewster's transgressions of form and discipline. A reimagined courtyard is carved with the hieroglyphs of timeless bodies, enlivening the passive caryatid column as stone-ages Venuses with convex bellies and ample bosoms. Through her designs, Brewster questions how we build our environment and what sentiments it is based around. Beyond providing built space, what kind of living does it facilitate? From

her choice of discipline to her choice of materials, she reflects not just what she finds beautiful, but where she seeks value. Underpinning such value is a desire for freedom; to build worlds through voice, to bridge a gap and lay a path for others to follow. This freedom is why she continues to call herself a designer. The environment she creates and the outlook she carries reflect an assertion of self-value that propels her path wherever she dares – a philosophy for design, and for living too. ■

Above: Detail of Negress chaise longue, 2010
Overleaf: Still from the film *Passages*, 2026

The body is something
I play with like any
other object – never
devoid of meaning.
It carries stories, but
it can also be taken
apart, reassembled.

This artwork was purchased by Simone Brewster's parents from
Shepherd's Bush market in the 1960s. It contributed to an environment
where Black diaspora heritage was celebrated. Some may associate
dark woods with 18th-century colonial fashions, but for Brewster they
evoke the West African sculptures of her childhood.

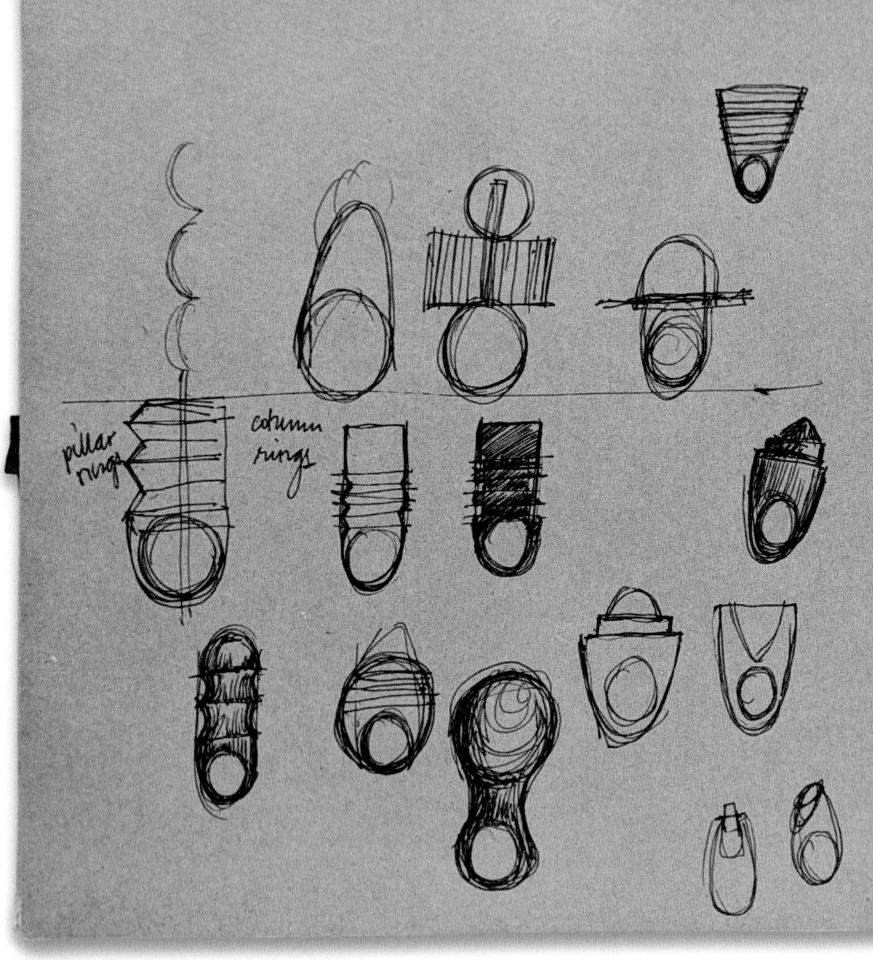

pillar rings
column rings

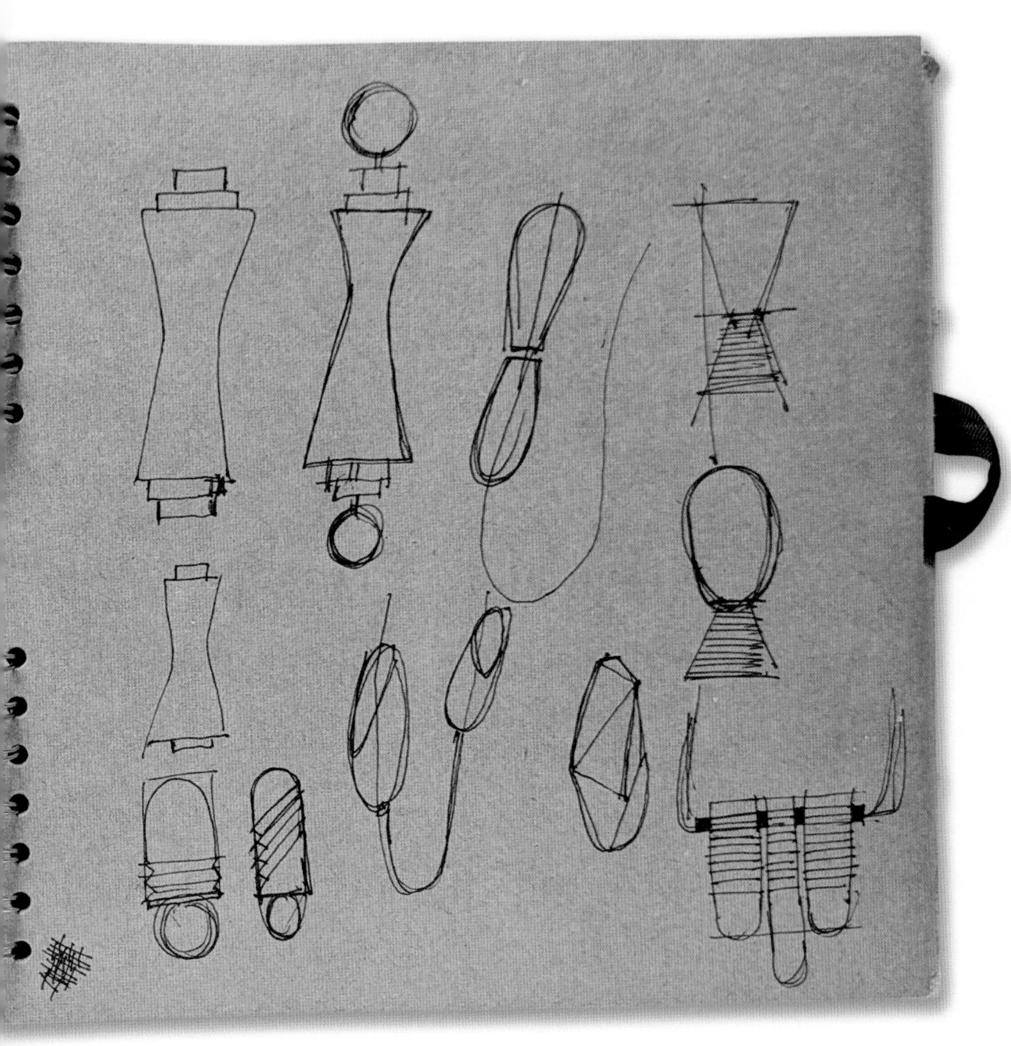

I considered a childish idea of what is precious, what is oversized, as a playful display of what you want people to see.

Brewster created this Ebony ring in 2009 from a repurposed sample from a Norfolk factory. This inspired her to produce the wood-based ring collection, 'Ebony Revolution'.

...ony revolution — cut woods to make them preciou..
-treat them like a precious &
- Qualities - layers/tones/ looks con
large statement simp
metropolis necklace

- NEW MATERIAL COPPER (WARM
- layers in the copper
  • CIRCLES.. • SEMI CIR
  • 'U' SHAPES • PRECIOUS P
             OF WOOD

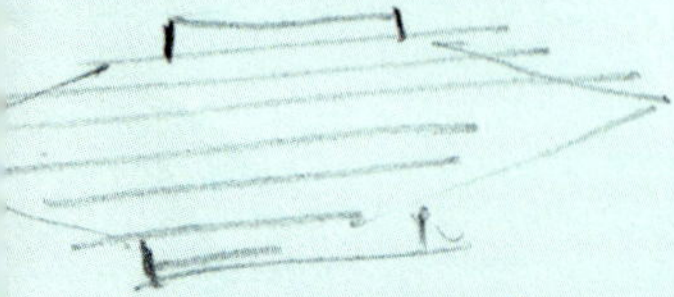

turned tangles

XTREME SHAPE
OLOUR BLACK

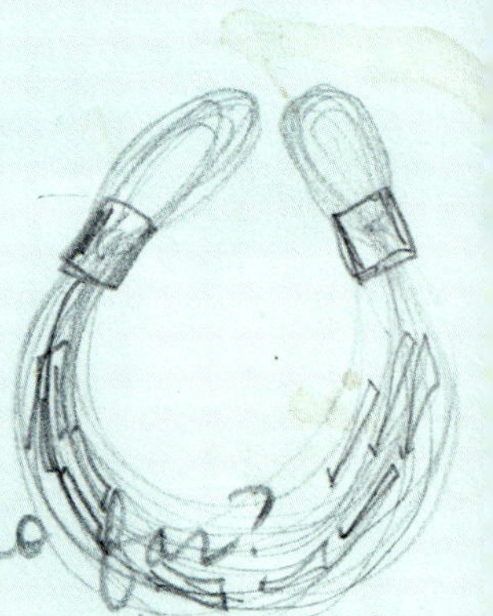

(3 NEW PIECES)

hat has not been considered so far?
The threads
The clasp

ONG CHAIN

long {

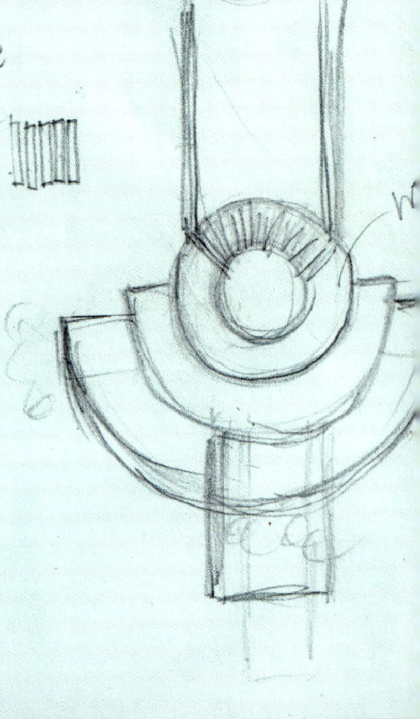

tube

OCCASION: OSCAR, DRESS

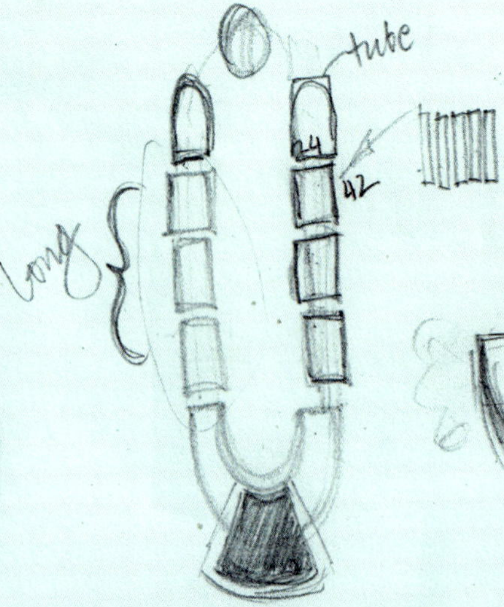

Above: Ebony Revolution necklace, 2010
Opposite: Ebony Revolution sketches, 2010

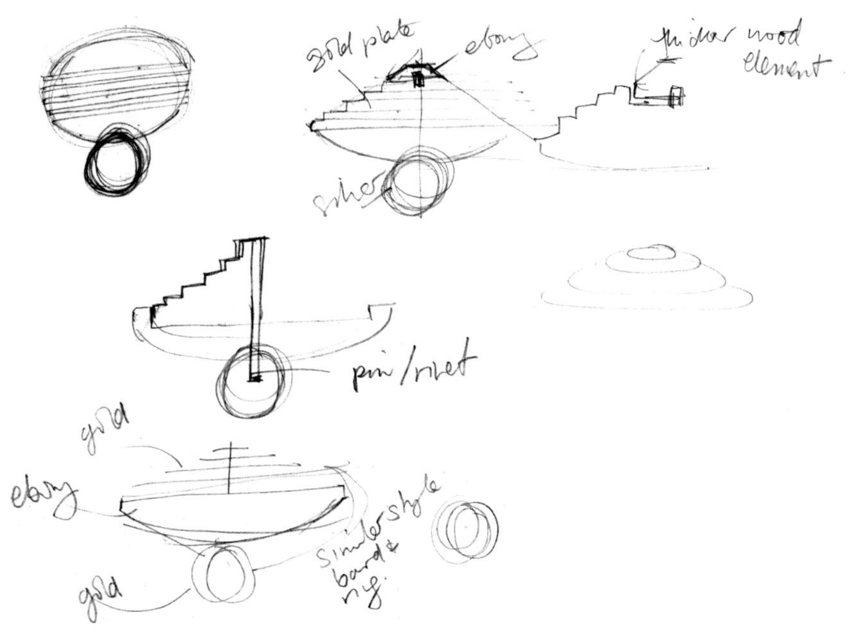

    Ebony Revolution sketches, 2009

Ebony Revolution conical ring, 2009

60   Totem bracelet, 2010

We can build a space
of just objects; we
don't need four walls
and a roof. Therefore
architecture can be
created through an
assemblage of objects.

    Turned wood elements, 2019, and conceptual sketches, 2010

64   Turned wood elements conceptual sketch, 2019

Turned wood elements conceptual sketch, 2019

Above: Turned wood element 1, 2019
66   Opposite: Turned wood element 2, 2019

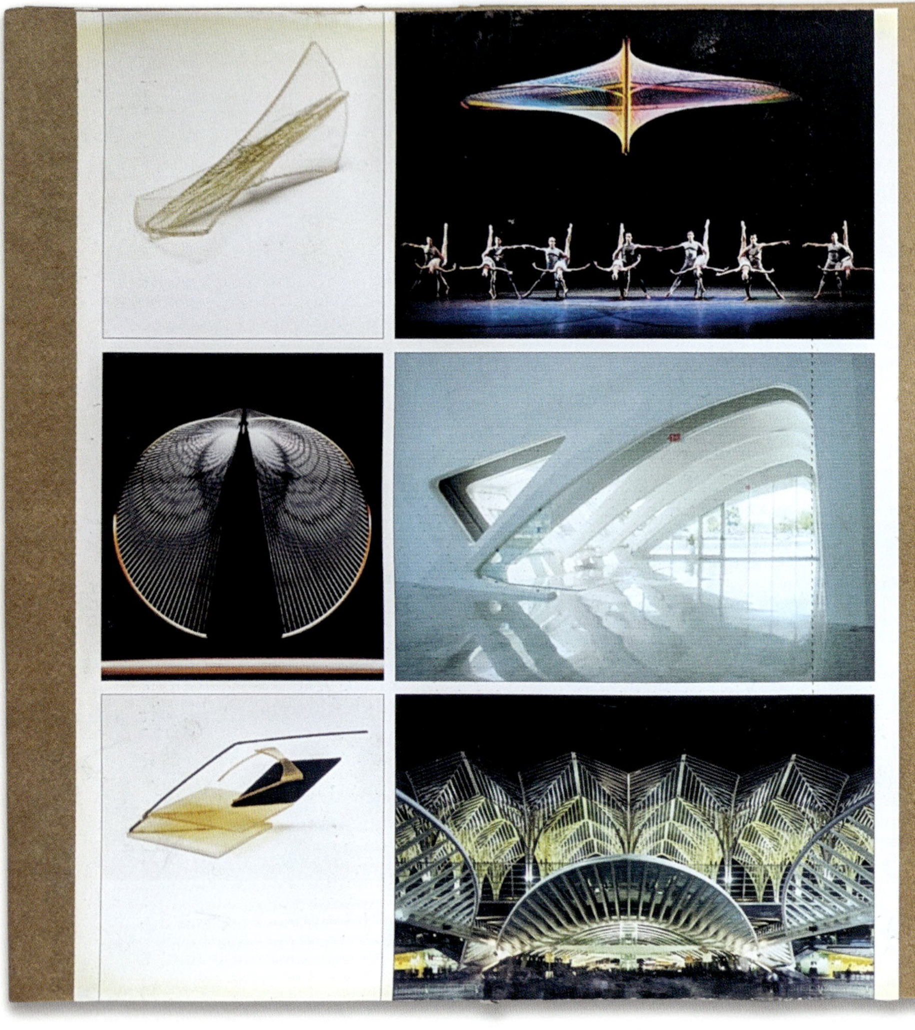

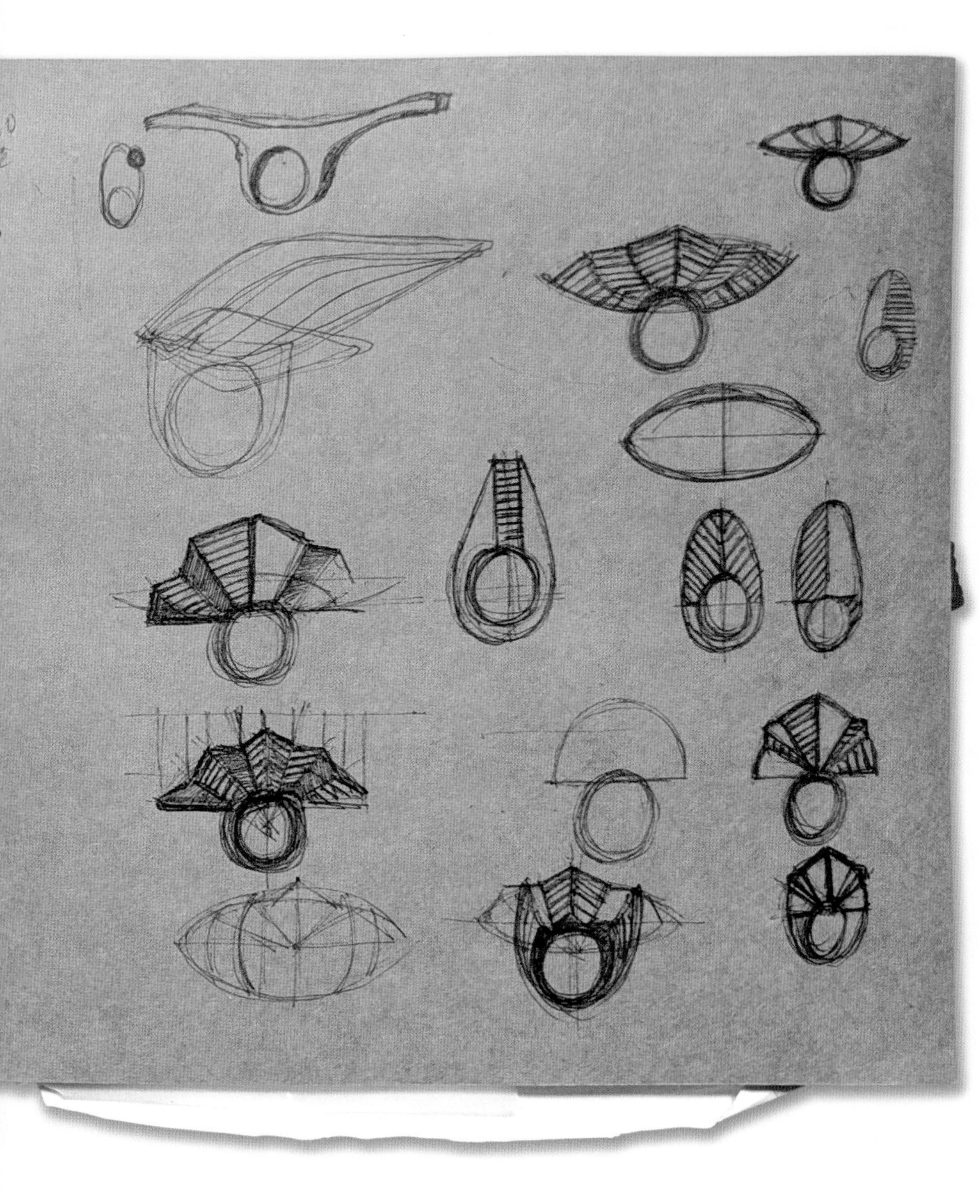

african
super
model

wood and glass

    Silver Metropolis, Large Sliced ring, 2015

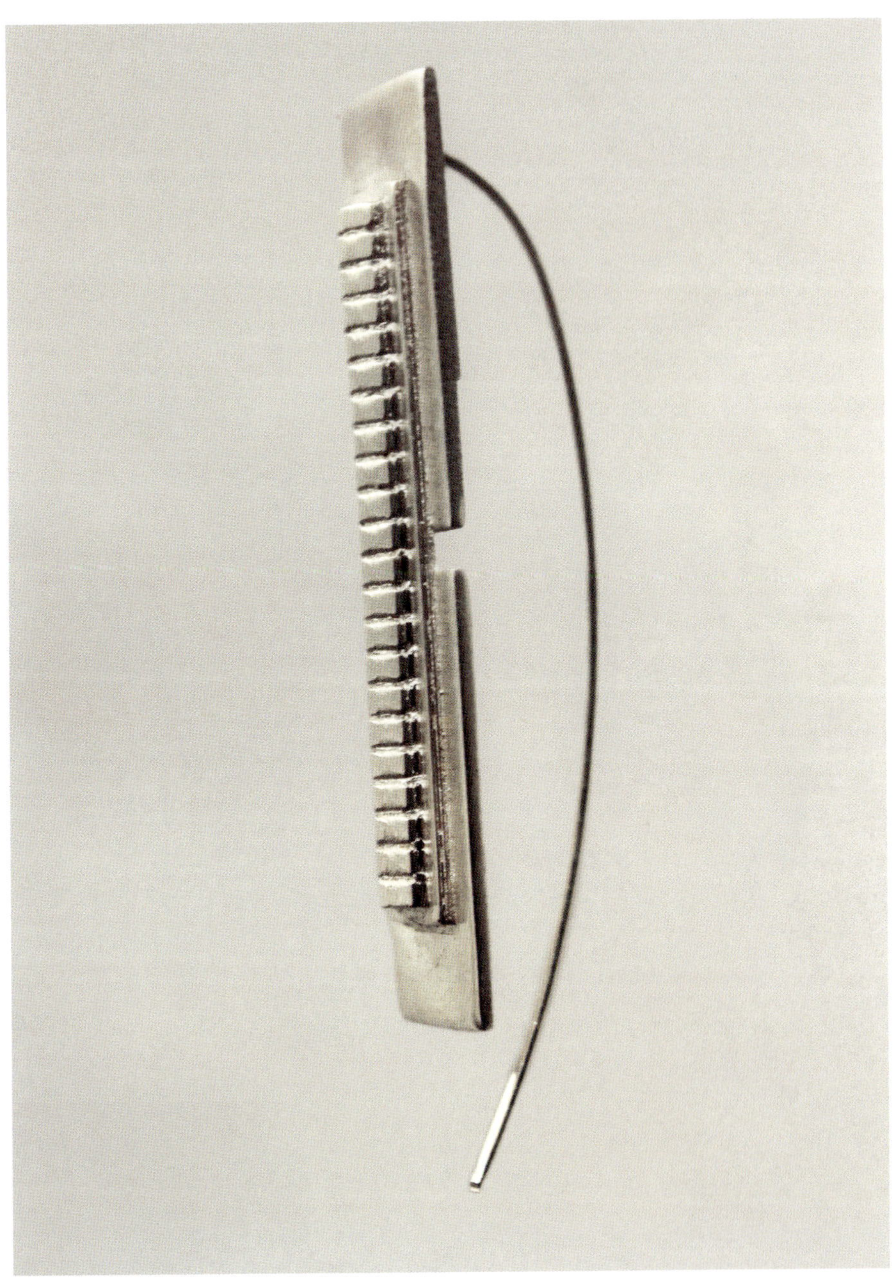

Silver Metropolis, Long Column earring, 2015

In Brewster's *Crown* series of 2023, each comb adopts exaggerated silhouettes of hairstyles specific to African tribes. The three-pronged comb draws on the striking, alluring silhouettes of Mangbetu royalty. The four-pronged comb represents the royalty of the Azande kingdom in modern-day Democratic Republic of Congo and South Sudan.

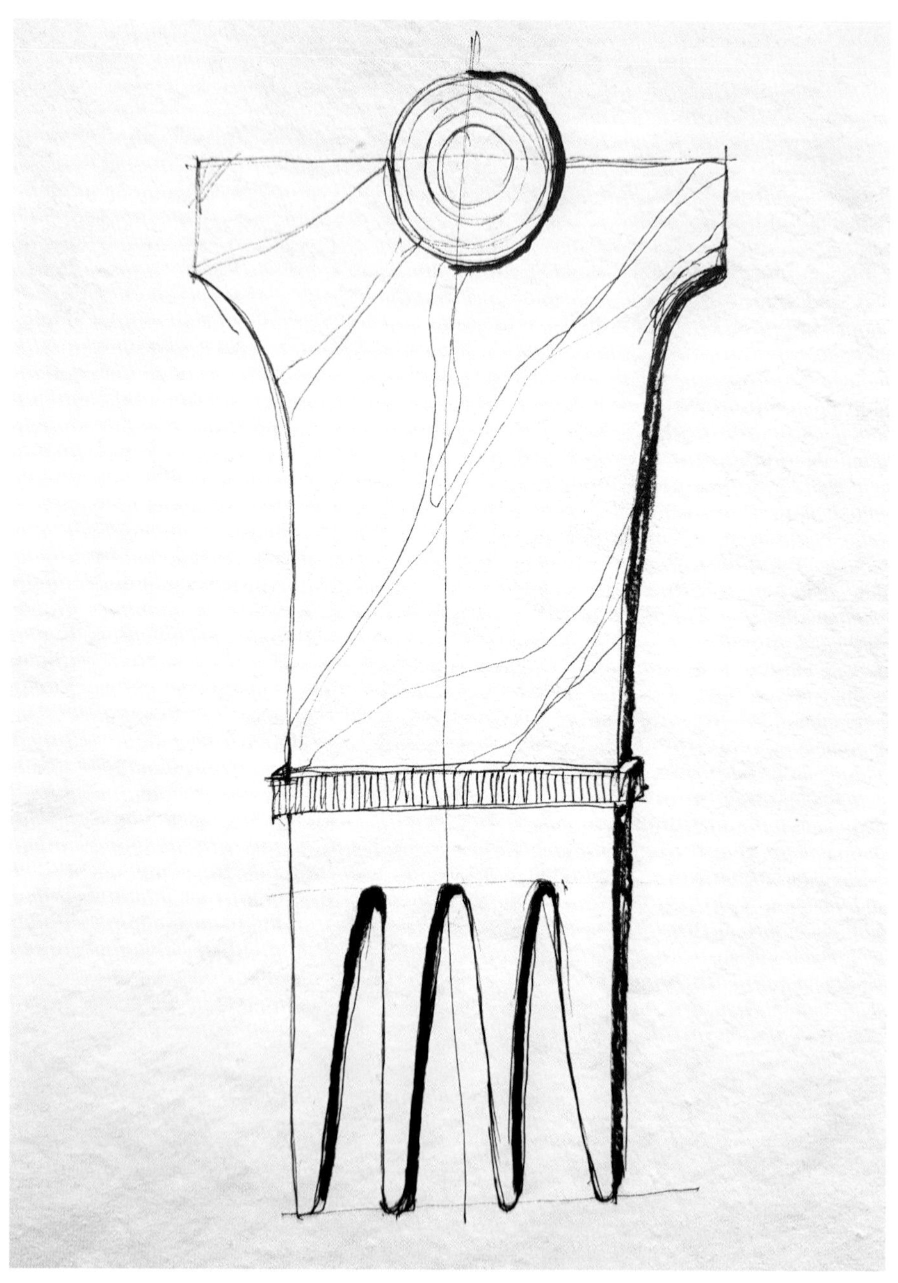

    Comb sketch, 2023

Three-pronged comb, 2023

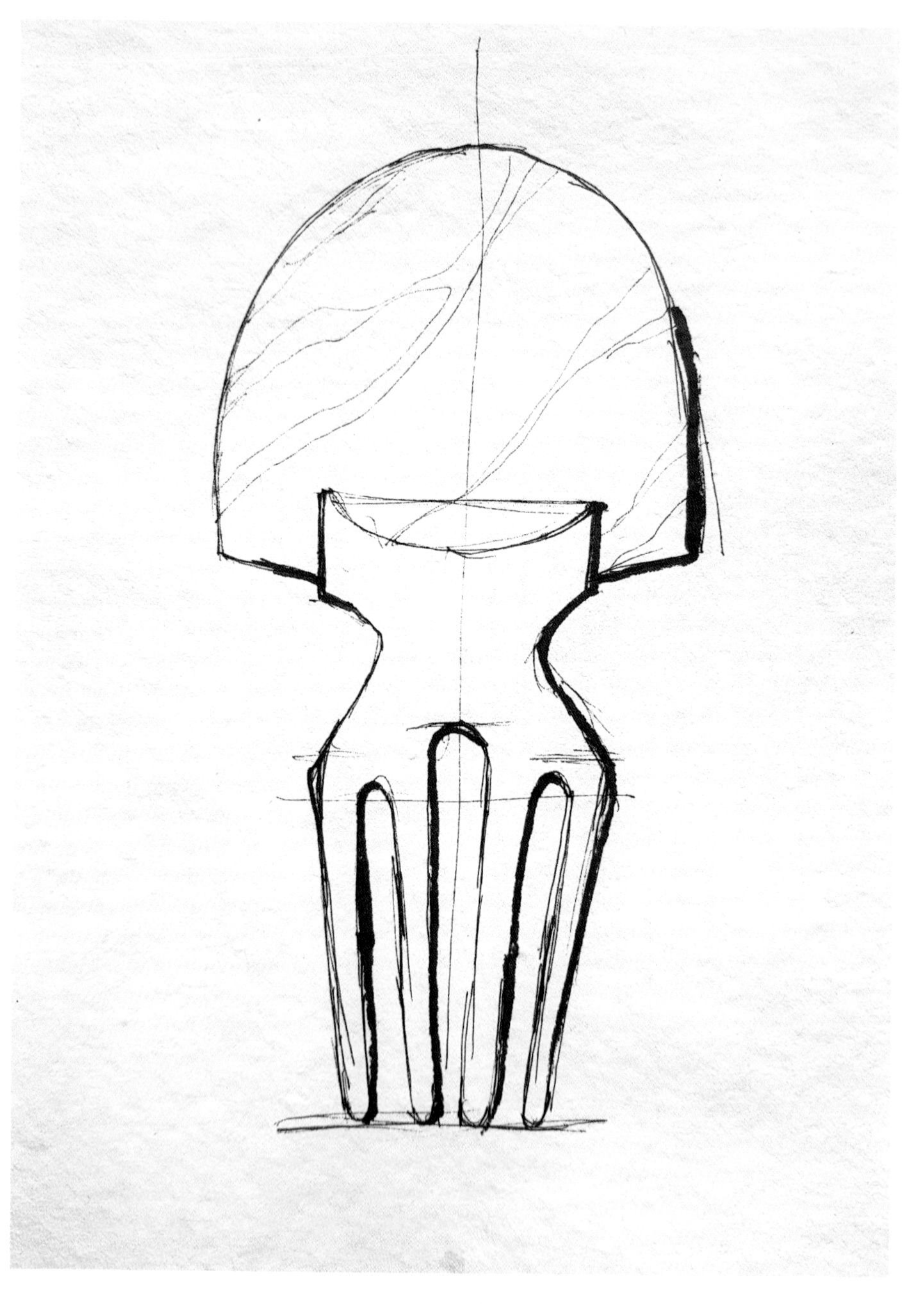

78   Comb sketch, 2023

Four-pronged comb, 2023

80   Five-pronged comb, 2023

For Heritage Three-Column necklace, 2023, Brewster uses hair-like
material to tap into the deep cultural associations of hair, using it both
as inspiration and material in jewellery designs.

82   Overleaf: Metropolis Grand necklace, 2015

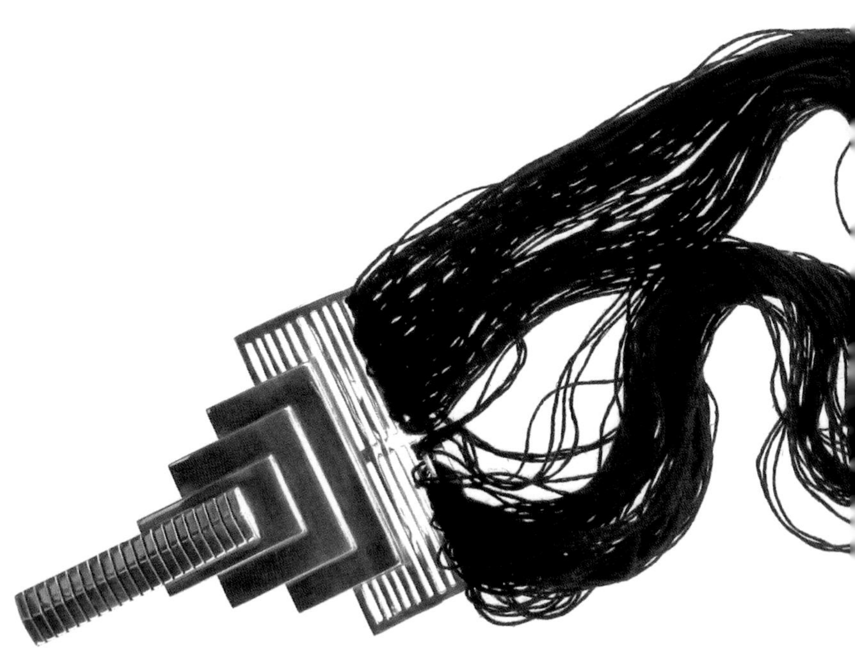

Shapes have power.
Shapes have history.
Name these shapes.

Opposite: Stepping stools, 2009
Overleaf: Strata planters, 2021

   Above and opposite: Concept sketches for Tropical Noire, 2014

With her *Spirit of Place* installation, Brewster sought to capture the essence of a cork forest. The title translates the ancient Roman concept of *genius loci*, meaning the spirit or character of a place. Inspired by the pale moss green of the trees in Portugal's Herdade de Rio Frio forest (shown here), Brewster transported the emotions she felt in their company – peace, calm and connectivity – to central London.

the New Forest

1

2

3

4

   Spirit of Place concept sketches, 2023

5
7

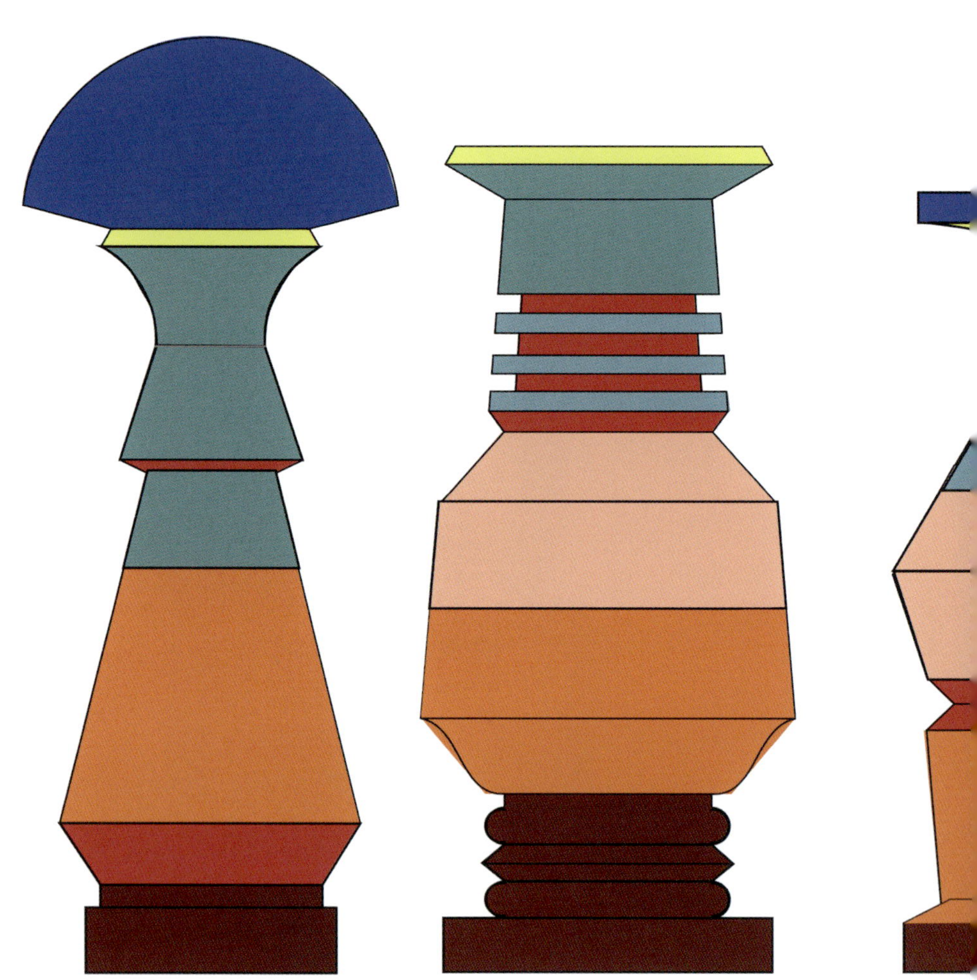

Spirit of Place, 2023

One sketch became a hieroglyphic in *Temple of Relics*, that idea was planted then...

Sketches of hieroglyphs for *Temple of Relics*, 2025. The walls of *Temple of Relics* are engraved with symbols which, from afar, resemble Egyptian hieroglyphs. Up close, they reveal abstracted female forms that echo Brewster's expressive paintings.

The murder of George Floyd in 2020 sparked collective outrage and galvanised the Black Lives Matter movement. In response, Brewster adapted the visual language of her painting series 'Woman in Parts' to examine Black male bodies' vulnerability to symbolic and objective violence in society. This poster features a lyrical poem by South African comedian Trevor Noah, which references the emotions around the protests surrounding George Floyd's death and the Colin Kaepernick kneeling movement that started in 2016.

It's wrong to do it in the streets,
It's wrong to do it in the tweets;
You cannot do it on the field,
You cannot do it if you kneeled;
And don't do it if you're rich!
You ungrateful son of a bitch;
Because there's one thing that's a fact
YOU CANNOT PROTEST IF YOU'RE
BLACK.

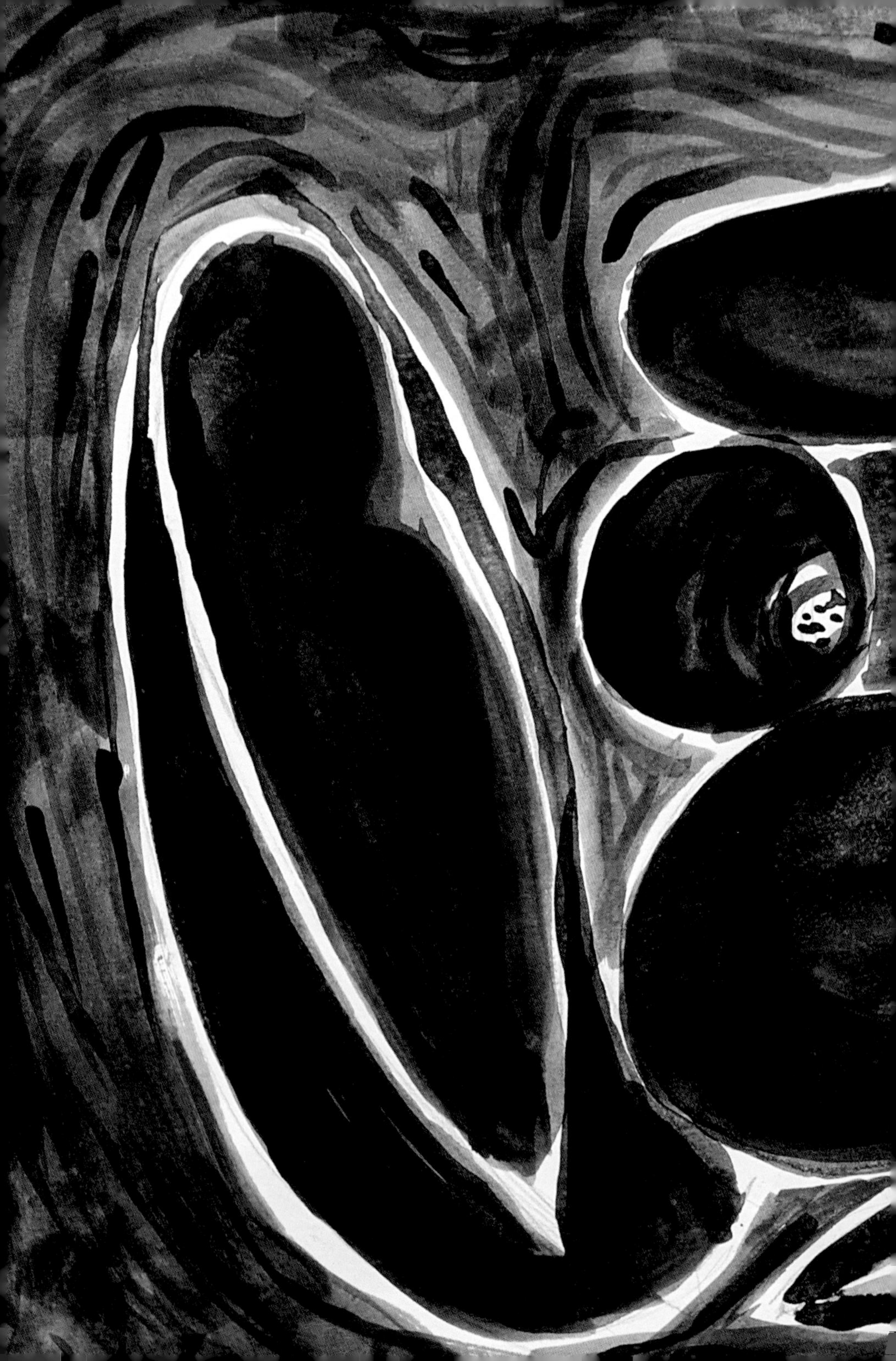

Previous page: *Assemblage* painting, 2020

 Opposite: *Bodyscape* painting, 2020

112   Detail of Negress chaise longue, 2025

'... Negress retains a quizzical stance no matter the setting, asking us to see ourselves in relation to bodies made strange or strangely familiar in Brewster's hands.'

(Michelle Joan Wilkinson, Curator of Architecture and Design, Smithsonian National Museum of African American History and Culture)

Negrita, 2025. The title derives from a historically racist Spanish term meaning 'little Black girl'. In contemporary Black communities, the term has been reclaimed to complement boldness. The gilded nipple, added to emphasise the double meaning in the name – both historical and reclaimed – affirms the subject's intrinsic value.

   Textile pattern for Jakke Coat design, 2021

    Woman in Parts, *Untitled 30*, 2020

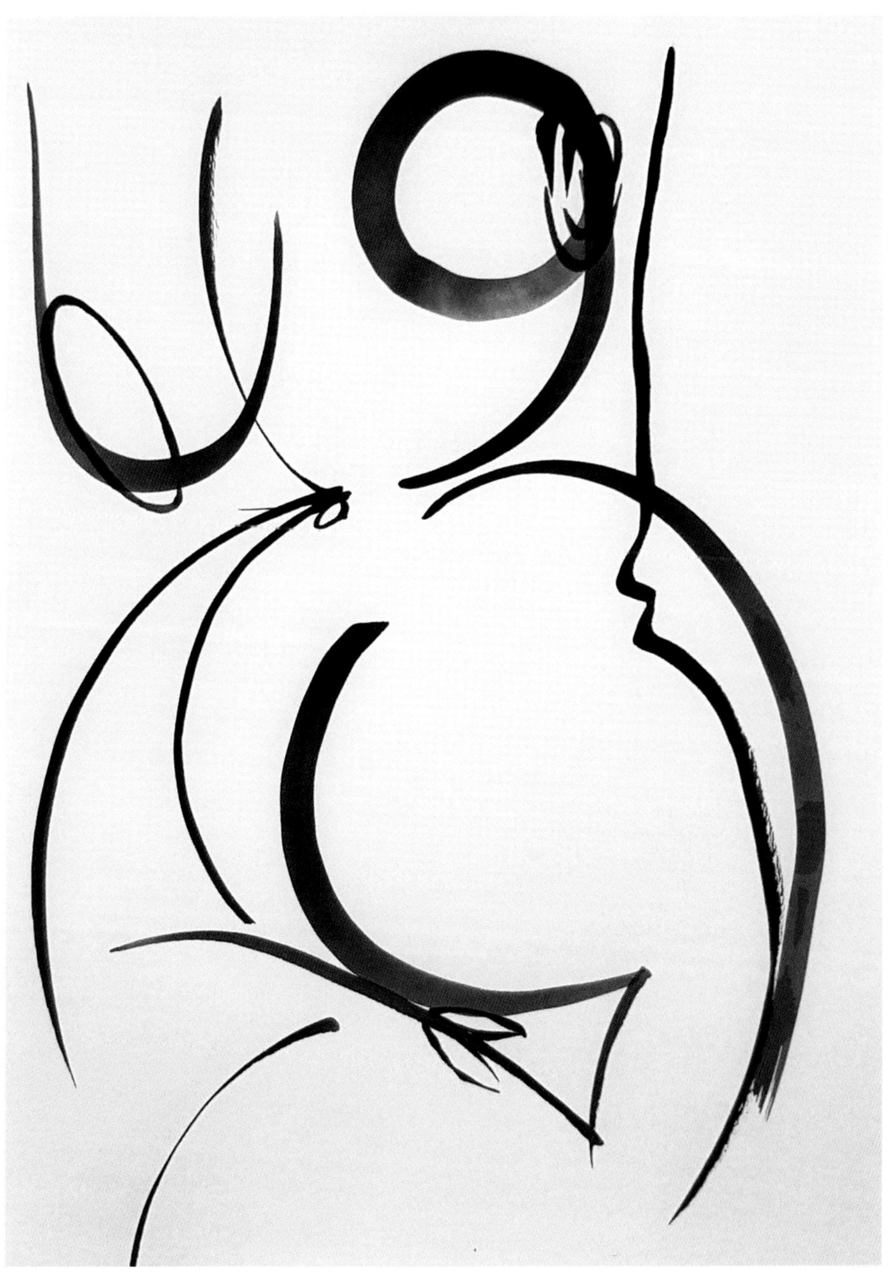

Woman in Parts, *Untitled 48*, 2020

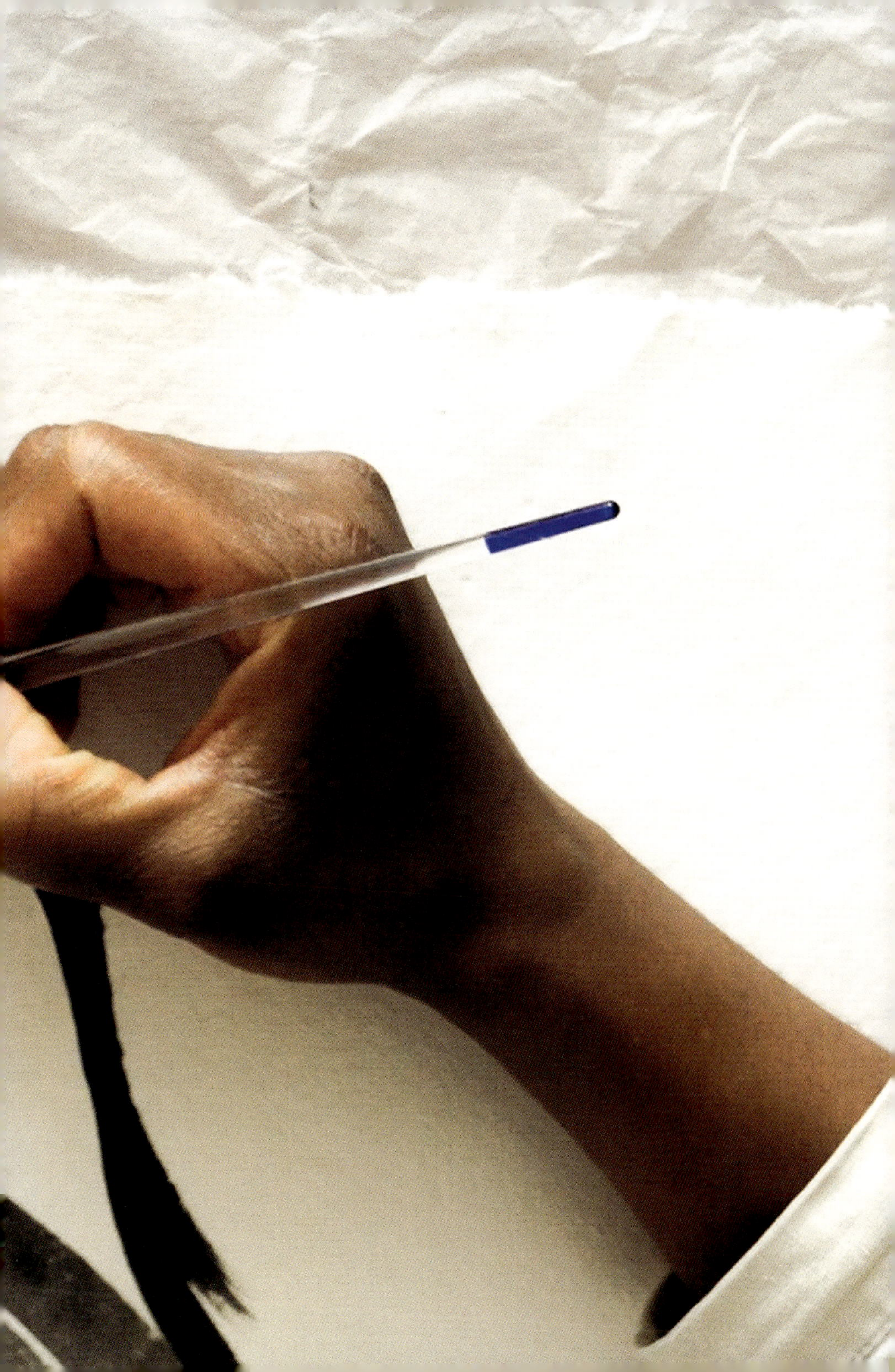

Previous page: Still from the film *Passages*, 2026
Opposite: Painted rug design for Roger Oates Design, 2025

Simone Brewster is a multi-disciplinary designer, whose work challenges the status quo of what is beautiful and valuable in institutional contexts. Having studied architecture at The Barlett School of Architecture, UCL, and obtained an MA in Design Products at the Royal College of Art, Brewster works across a range of scales and disciplines, defying hasty categorisation. She plays with form, experimenting with material understanding and exploration, employing a visual language that is architectural and sculptural. Her designs are rich with material histories and layered with references, from palaeolithic fertility deities to West African diaspora traditions. She has been commissioned by international partners including London Design Festival, Habitat, Liberty Fabrics and Amorim Cork. Her works have been acquired in the UK by the Museum of London (re-launched as the London Museum in 2026), the Victoria and Albert Museum, London, and the Walker Art Gallery, Liverpool, and in the US by the Smithsonian National Museum of African American Art and Culture, Washington D.C.

The second PLATFORM display at the Design Museum was dedicated to Brewster's practice and ran from 13 February 2026 to 25 January 2027.

Biographies

Thomas Aquilina is an architect and academic dedicated to building communities of radical imagination and collective practice. He is an Associate Professor and co-director of Spatial Justice at The Bartlett School of Architecture, UCL. His current research draws on diasporic spatial experiences in both global and local contexts from downtown Kingston in Jamaica to North Kensington in London.

Hadeel Eltayeb is a curator, writer and oral historian focused on identity and cultural production. She is Displays Curator at the Design Museum, leading on the annual PLATFORM and the Ralph Saltzman Prize displays. She has recently contributed to *The Architectural Review*, *Wes Anderson: The Archives* and *Tim Burton: Designing Worlds*.

Danielle Thom is a curator, writer, broadcaster and lecturer with a focus on contemporary craft and design, and on eighteenth-century sculpture and decorative arts. Currently Senior Curator at the Design Museum, Thom was previously Curator of Making at the London Museum (2017–22).

Picture credits

Every reasonable attempt has been made to identify owners of copyright. Errors and omissions notified to the publisher will be corrected in subsequent editions.

Unless otherwise stated, all images are © Courtesy Simone Brewster.

Background cover: Charles Emerson; pp. 1, 4: Ed Reeve; p. 8: Kevin C Moore; pp. 11, 14-5: Charles Emerson; p. 18: James Marshall; p. 22: © Chris Ofili. Courtesy the artist, Victoria Miro and David Zwirner; pp. 24-5: Juan Carlos Verona; pp. 29, 32-3: David Parry/PA Media Assignments; p. 38: Centre Pompidou, MNAM-CCI, Dist. GrandPalaisRmn/Georges Meguerditchian. © 2026 Wifredo Lam Estate, ADAGP, Paris and DACS, London; pp. 40, 43, 45: Charles Emerson; pp. 46-7: James Marshall; pp. 55, 60, 75, 79, 80-1, 83, 84-5: Charles Emerson; p. 88-9: Courtesy Areaware; pp. 92-3: Charles Emerson; p. 95: James Marshall; p. 101: Ed Reeve; p. 112: Kevin C Moore; pp. 120-1: James Marshall.

Acknowledgements

The Design Museum would like to express its sincere thanks to Simone Brewster and all of her collaborators who have shared their time, work and knowledge with us: Andrew Humber (The Whitewall), Charles Emerson, James Marshall (The Inventive), Kevin C. Moore, Samantha Williams (Brookfield Properties) and Séan Wild (Cloud & Horse).

We would like to acknowledge the dedication of Susanna Pousette Okudzeto, Emilie Foyer, Nana Biamah-Ofosu (YAA Projects) and Amandine Forest-Aguié in making the PLATFORM exhibition and this publication possible. The museum would like to give special thanks to transport partner Cadogan Tate.

We are also grateful to Walker Art Gallery, OXO Gallery Courtyard, Coin Street, PURPLE PR, and Michelle Joan Wilkinson, Curator of Architecture and Design at the Smithsonian National Museum of African American History and Culture.

Design Museum Publishing
Design Museum Enterprises Ltd
224–228 Kensington High Street
London W8 6AG
United Kingdom

Designmuseum.org

First published in 2026
© 2026 Design Museum Publishing

ISBN 978-1-872005-88-1

Printed by Park Communications Ltd,
Alpine Way, London

Inside cover: Detail from Totem
Grand bracelet, 2010
p.1: Detail from Spirit of Place
pillar, 2023
p.4: View of Spirit of Place
installation, 2023

Senior Publishing Manager
Miranda Harrison

Publishing Manager
Stefano Mancin

Editors
Miranda Harrison
Hadeel Eltayeb

Designer
Stefano Mancin

Picture Editor
Anabel Navarro

Series Design
Daly & Lyon

Distribution

Worldwide excluding USA
and Canada:
Thames & Hudson
181A High Holborn
London WC1V 7QX
United Kingdom
Thamesandhudson.com

North America:
ARTBOOK | D.A.P
75 Broad Street, Suite 630
New York, NY10004
United States of America
www.artbook.com